YOUNG ROUTEMASTERS

James Whiting

Capital Transport

Above: Brand new RM 1 on the tilt test at Chiswick works.

Front cover: The 48 was one of the routes introduced in November 1959 at the first stage of the trolleybus replacement to use Routemasters. It went beyond the trolleybus terminus at Aldgate to provide a new link to Waterloo. RM 127 is seen at St Paul's.

Opposite: Route 67 was introduced at stage 11 of trolleybus replacement. RM 836 was one of 55 RMs allocated to Stamford Hill at this stage.

Title page: RM 335 was initially allocated to Shepherds Bush at stage seven of the trolleybus replacement programme in July 1960 but transferred to Walthamstow in November that year. All the RMs originally allocated to the 256 were of the non-opening upper deck front window design. Across the road is the distinctive stonework on the entrance to Bunhill Fields.

First published 2020

ISBN 978-1-85414-450-8

Published by Capital Transport Publishing Ltd
www.capitaltransport.com

Author's Note

My own introduction, as a primary school pupil, to the existence of the Routemaster was by way of issue 49 of *The Beezer* comic, published on 20th December 1956, which on the back page had an illustrated feature of London motor buses through the years. It included a rather rough drawing of RM 1 which made it look like a lowbridge bus. The artist had captured the lower front and bonnet area well but it looked as though he might have had to rush the rest to meet a deadline. Had I been into Meccano, I may have seen the issue of the Meccano Magazine for that August, which had an excellent hand-coloured photo of RM 1 on the cover, but I was not and did not. The Ian Allan ABC first showed the Routemaster on the cover of its eleventh edition, which appeared in the early part of 1955. This too had passed me by.

All this provides a sharp contrast to today's plentiful information whereby nothing escapes attention and all of us can be very well informed of all developments. It was the newness of the design of RM 1 that impressed me, particularly the frontal treatment, though others took a different view. Indeed some, like the late Ken Glazier, were very disappointed on first sight of RM 1 in view of its boxy appearance. Seeing it at the 1954 Commercial Motor Show, he said he was 'frankly dismayed' by the very upright front and what he felt was a 'too bulky' bonnet design. Ken Blacker also was disappointed with the 'boxy' bus when he first saw it at Golders Green on its first day in service in February 1956. He and some friends rode on it to the other end of route 2, Crystal Palace, to find that the seats were less comfortable than on the RT, the interior design was more angular and austere and what should have been a plus point on that cold February day, the heating system, was not working. The heating was to continue to prove troublesome.

I find the first years of Routemaster operation particularly fascinating and know I am not alone in this, hence this book. The book records RM introduction, in route order, and so covers the period from 1956 up to the last conversions using new buses in the first half of 1965. Being a routes based story, the main batch of red RMLs is not included because with just one exception (the 104A) these all entered service on routes previously operated with RMs.

Many good friends generously assisted with information for this book including (in alphabetical order) Laurie Akehurst, Tony Beard, Ken Blacker, Jim Hawkins, Chris Holland, Andrew Morgan, Colin Stannard and Bob Williamson, some of whom also kindly checked the proofs, as did ever-helpful Mike Lloyd. I thank John Marshall for sending me digital copies of all the Chiswick daily records of vehicle movements for the period. Providing much valuable help with photographs have been Malcolm Papes, Tony Belton, John and Carole Gascoine, Jim Hawkins, Peter Jones, Gerald Mead, Robin Newell and Colin Stannard. Photograph retouching and restoration work where needed has been expertly carried out by Mike Eyre. Without all these people the book could not have been compiled.

James Whiting
July 2020

Opposite: The first prototype at its first trade press showing in August 1954. Chief Mechanical Engineer A A M Durrant is among those on the platform and is standing on the right.

RM 1 was built at London Transport's Chiswick works with major design input on the body design by industrial designer Douglas Scott. A mock-up was completed at Chiswick in the spring of 1952 and the final version was approved in May 1953, particular attention being given to the radiator grille design. The final grille design on the mock-up was based on a suggestion by a member of the LTE board, Alexander Valentine, who later became the Executive's chairman. The building of the body then began. On 26th August, at one of Chief Mechanical Engineer for Road Services Bill Durrant's regular meetings, consideration was given to finishing one of the prototypes in unpainted aluminium. Though consideration did not continue up to the point where the actual vehicle was identified there are some grounds for thinking it would have been RML 3. The unpainted bus idea was not forgotten but it was eight years before an RM appeared in this condition. RM 1 was first shown to the trade press at Chiswick on 25th August 1954 in advance of its inclusion in the 1954 Earls Court Commercial Motor Show the following month. No transfers have been applied in this view and a name had not yet been thought of for the new bus; it was chosen a few days before the Earls Court Show. This view, showing the offside route number plate holder originally fitted, is at the Chiswick press preview. The absence of wheel trim may have been for a good reason but it did detract from its appearance.

RM 1 entered service on route 2 (Golders Green to Crystal Palace) from Cricklewood garage on Wednesday 8th February 1956. It was nearly ten years earlier, on 24th September 1946, that Durrant first asked the LPTB chairman Lord Ashfield for a budget of £2500 to cover a start on development work for a bus of chassisless construction; a proposal that in due course was to result in the Routemaster. Cooling problems led to the underfloor radiator on RM 1 being removed later in 1956 after returning to Chiswick in August for a conventional front radiator to be fitted and also a later design of engine (AV590), which had not been available when RM 1 was first built. This engine then became standard on AEC RMs. That same month, the British Transport Commission gave London Transport authorisation to buy 1520 Routemasters for trolleybus replacement. The number eventually used for this purpose was some way below this figure, later vehicles from this sanction being used for RT replacement or supplied as RMCs. Indeed by May 1959, even before RMs began to be used for trolleybus replacement routes, the estimate of the type needed for that purpose had reduced by 431 to 1089. There was more than one factor at work in this. First, the initial three stages of trolleybus replacement used RT family buses and there had been substantial service cuts following the 1958 bus strike. The maximum number of scheduled trolleybuses immediately before the bus strike had been 1434. RM 1 was the first London bus to have interior heating.

RM 1 was returned to Cricklewood with its new engine and frontal appearance in February 1957 and re-entered service in March. By today's standards the maximum length for a two-axle double decker bus in the mid-1950s seems rather small at 27 feet, the length of RM 1 in its original condition. The revised frontal design on RM 1 (which RM 2 entered service with) gave a revised length of 27ft 4ins and coincided with an increase in a revised legal length of 27ft 6ins. The modified RM 1 is seen in Edgware Road in the summer of 1957. The bus in this form was used on route 260 (Colindale to Waterloo) on Mondays to Saturdays (extended to Surrey Docks, Mon-Fri peaks) and route 2 on Sundays. These RM prototypes were not popular with conductors as they were usually put onto the same duty everyday. Some regular passengers and especially school children would wait for them in preference to the preceding RT. This, coupled with the eight additional seats, meant that the conductors were doing more work. RM 1 continued in service until the beginning of December 1959, but did not see service again after then and was demoted to training duties later that month.

London Transport was obliged to order part of its new bus requirements from Leyland Motors and so two of the prototypes had Leyland mechanical units and 9.8 litre engines. Of these, RML 3 was sent to Willesden in January 1958 and remained there, apart from a two-month absence following an accident, until November 1959. The accident, which was neither the fault of the bus driver nor the bus, gave some useful experience of how the front end stood up to impact and the engineers at Chiswick seemed generally pleased with its robustness in this respect following a heavy impact from a lorry. RML 3 was the only Routemaster to be bodied by Weymann. It was demoted to training duties in November 1959 and renumbered RM 3 in August 1961 to make the class letters available for the lengthened Routemasters. The first production RM to be fitted with a Leyland engine was RM 632 in September 1961 and so RML 3 was the only Leyland RM bus to be distinguished for a time with a different class code.

RM 2 was identical in almost all respects to RM 1 except that, to provide comparisons in fuel consumption and performance, it had a smaller engine; a 7.7 litre AV470 as opposed to the 9.6 litre A204. It was initially intended to run it in the Central area, route 3 being selected for it. Following its being taken into stock in grey primer in March 1955, the bus went through a period of extensive testing that turned out rather longer than had been planned. The bus was not placed in passenger service until May 1957, by which time it had been fitted with a 9.6 litre engine following testing and it had been decided to paint it green and send it to the Country area. It failed to impress there however, with Geoffrey Fernyhough, the department's manager, feeling that the bus was too sophisticated. He campaigned instead for a new Country bus with platform doors, using a 'more austere' steel body on RM subframes, a different gearbox and a smaller engine. He felt that doored designs then being placed into service by other companies, notably southern neighbour Southdown, were superior for his needs to the RM. Durrant responded by saying that he did not envisage RT replacement on bus routes in the Country area starting until 1968. The discussions were to lead to heaters being fitted to all Country bus RTs within a few years.

CRL 4 was the prototype Routemaster for Green Line, the third in a series of double decker prototypes for these cross-London express services after LT 1137 and RTC 1. There was a keenness to have more of these as early as possible but not at the expense of deliveries for trolleybus replacement, which was the number one priority at the time. In March 1956 however it was felt it would be possible to have 60 coach Routemasters in 1958 for the Romford and Grays Green Line routes. This proved over-optimistic. In September 1958 Durrant asked whether Park Royal might be able to supply 16 coach Routemasters for a cross-London route in 1959 (at the rate of one per week) without any effect on RM deliveries. Although the response has not been seen, the likely reply is that it would not be in view of the fact that no more coach Routemasters followed until just after the trolleybus programme was completed. The option of using ECW and/or Leyland, if considered at all, was not followed. CRL 4, which became RMC 4 in August 1961, had a very good life in passenger service and last operated in May 1979. All three other prototypes were withdrawn by the end of 1959. This view is at North Finchley in 1961 soon after reclassification to RMC and while it was painted in an experimental lighter green livery. The vehicle had entered service on 9th October 1957 on route 721.

When the trolleybus conversion programme was being planned, there was at one point the intention to convert one route in advance of the rest to obtain some service experience with the new Routemaster. Route 698 was initially identified as being a suitable route for this trial, but this later changed to 654 and then changed again to 611 when it was felt that a more arduous route would be better. In August 1957 these ideas were superseded by an intention to use the first production vehicles on existing bus routes. At this time Durrant reported that there had been delays in supplying PRV with RM drawings that would result in 'RM deliveries in 1958 being put back two months'. Then, in 1958 there were major delays in production getting under way. Only one bus was completed in 1958, this being RM 8, which was made ready for display at that year's Commercial Motor Show at Earls Court which opened in September. Because of the delays in the delivery of the new buses, it was not until 11th May 1959 that the first production RM was received into stock, this being RM 6. Two more (RMs 9 and 11) followed nine days later. For the trials on a number of existing RT family bus routes passing through central London. In the first five days of June, by when more RMs had been received, eleven were sent to garages for training and then immediate service use. Six entered service that month: three from Willesden (RMs 5, 7 and 24) and one each from Riverside (14), Hackney (18) and Cricklewood (19). Hackney's RM was originally intended for Battersea, which shared route 22, but the accommodation there was found to be unsuitable for RMs. The buses ran as extras with special schedules. At the time there were restrictions on which routes could operated 8ft wide buses, so the routes selected were those which had an allocation either of RTWs or one of the prototypes. RM 18 is seen in Holborn.

A further 13 RMs entered service in July 1959. Three of them went to increase Willesden's allocation to six and five more went to each of Riverside and Cricklewood. The routes involved were 8 (and 8B Sundays) from Willesden, 11 (and 27 Sundays) from Riverside and 260 weekdays (and 2 Sundays) from Cricklewood, at which RM 1 was already at work. Hackney continued with its single RM which was used on route 22. Representing the operation from Willesden is RM 25 at Bishopsgate on the Monday to Saturday working. Many, mostly minor, problems were reported during the time these first buses were in service. These included leakages from the hydraulic brakes and air systems, wheel nuts not being fully tightened (in some cases missing), and problems with window wipers, all affecting a number of vehicles. Individual and more serious problems occurred with RM 24, which had braking problems that were found to be caused by poor assembly of brake components. RM 5 needed its flywheel renewed after only a short time in service owing to a damaged component. RM 47 was involved in an accident caused by the failure of an electro-pneumatic unit. Accidents were more frequent with the new buses than with RTs during the same period, but this was largely attributed by the engineers to driver unfamiliarity with them. In April Durrant had stated that it was essential that District Engineers should regard themselves as personally responsible for preparing reports of the RM's performance in service and that they should also 'without fail' make a point of travelling each week on the vehicles under their control. The 'terrible twins' front posters were carried by almost all of these RMs in trial service and many early RMs carried them in the early period of trolleybus replacement also. Whereas the prototypes had destination binds with four lines of via points all the production buses had three lines, much improving readability.

The production RMs at Cricklewood joined RM 1 during its second spell of service there. RM 39 is seen leaving Cricklewood Lane being followed by a doomed trolleybus. On 26th August 1959 a two-man team from Chiswick Works went to Cricklewood to ride on three of its RMs (10, 39 and 42) to check the effectiveness of the upper deck ventilation. There had been some letters from passengers about the lack of front opening windows. To replace opening windows here, there were ventilation slots above each of the two windows, two grilles at waist level and three at floor level. Observations were made of and in the front seats. The weather on the day was fine and sunny with a slight breeze and with temperatures in the range 70-80 degrees Fahrenheit. The engineers found the ventilation satisfactory, reporting that: 'When the vehicle was moving a steady flow of air was maintained through the grilles. At no time was the air stuffy although the direct sunlight through the windows was warm. Cigarette smoke in the area cleared gradually but within reasonable time.' The report concluded that: 'No discomfiture on the part of other passengers sitting in the front seats was noticed'. The new bonnet design was not ideal aesthetically and the body's designer, Douglas Scott, who I was fortunate enough to be in touch with some years ago, told me in a letter 'The top line of the bonnet had to be modified to accommodate everything, giving it that broken backed appearance which has become so familiar that no-one notices it except me'.

Opposite: Another July entry into service was RM 32 at Riverside on what for many years was regarded as the key bus route for tourists. It displays at the front one of the cryptic adverts of the time for London Transport advertising, this one suggesting that children can be targeted by adverts on buses – a message perhaps aimed at sugary cereal and sweet manufacturers. The smartly turned out RM has clearly not been in service for long in this view. The following month, when works holidays slowed down deliveries, Hackney received another RM for its share of the 22 and another went to Turnham Green for the 91 (27 on Sundays), joining RM 2 there. Only two other RMs were added to those licensed for service that month, these going to Cricklewood to increase its allocation to eight.

The major delays in deliveries meant that the first three conversions of trolleybus routes had to be carried out using RTs and RTLs. By August 1959 the third stage had been reached using these vehicle types, many made spare following route withdrawals after the 1958 bus strike. September saw another 13 RMs entering service on major bus routes, including six to Tottenham, its first. These were for use on route 76. Whether any also got on to Brimsdown power station route 34B, a peak hour works service which took its buses from the 76 allocation, is unlikely. Special schedules for these extras were supplied by 55 Broadway with a view to central London operation as typified by RM 56 on Westminster Bridge.

Opposite: With RMs programmed to enter service in quantity the following month, October added one more RM to Willesden, four more to Turnham Green, including RM 96, and one more to Hackney. RM 101 is seen on the Sunday operation of route 27 at Hammersmith and was one of fifty RMs to have rear-axle air suspension fitted as a trial with three different types later in 1959. My own recollection of this was that on some of the vehicles the air suspension could cause travel sickness. No more were done. On the four prototypes the fuel tank had been on the nearside, as on the RT, but for better balancing of wheel loadings the production buses had the tank on the offside. RMs 1 and 2 and RML 3 ran alongside the production RMs in their service testing period. RM 2, now red, continued in passenger service until November and is seen at Turnham Green having just left its garage.

On the roads, the M1 motorway was just over a week old. In space, two months earlier, Russia had been the first country to have a rocket reach the moon. On the railways an extensive modernisation programme was in progress for the elimination of steam. All this formed part of the backdrop to the start of Routemasters taking over from trolleybuses on 11th November 1959. Route 5 replaced routes 567 and 665 and was shared between Poplar and West Ham garages, PR having the greater share. RM 113 is seen at the Bloomsbury end of the route. The Clerkenwell Green to Limehouse section of the route was also covered by a Monday to Friday 5A, which had a short spur at Limehouse to terminate at West India Docks. The lowest route number used in the trolleybus conversion programme, 5 had been released five years earlier on the withdrawal of a short, and short lived, local route between Shepherds Bush and Ladbroke Grove.

The 284 was the first RM night route and covered part of daytime route 5. The route number lasted under a year as from 11th October 1960 it became N84 as part of the general renumbering of night routes in preparation for having more route numbers available for trolleybus replacement services.

Though part of stage four of the trolleybus replacement programme, the 238 was principally a replacement for bus route 23B (Becontree Heath to Barking) with an extension from Barking to Canning Town to supplement 567/665 replacement route 5 along this section. In Monday to Friday peak hours it was also extended from Canning Town to North Woolwich to supplement new route 48 between these points. Operation was shared between Poplar and West Ham garages and had an initial allocation of 11 buses, giving the route a ten-minute frequency, increased to eight minute intervals in peak hours. The previous route with this number, running between Emerson Park and Noak Hill, had been withdrawn as part of the bus service cuts that followed the 1958 bus strike. It was these cuts that made the decision possible to use route numbers in the 1-299 series for replacement routes rather than former trolleybus route numbers. About half of the trial RMs on central London bus routes were withdrawn by or on 10th November and the other half had been taken off this work by 11th December, the last being RM 35 at Cricklewood. RM 2 and RML 3 had been withdrawn on 1st November, while RM 1 continued at work until the beginning of December. This first mass introduction of Routemasters (63 to Poplar including four spares and 15 to West Ham with just one spare) was far from smooth as detailed by Ken Blacker in *The Birth of the Routemaster* book. Breakdowns in service were common in the first weeks and pre-service checks at Aldenham were tightened up as extra spares were drafted in. Reporting on the position for the week ending 22nd December, Kenneth Shave stated that defects were still being found on new vehicles at the two garages. As an example, 12 of Poplar's RMs had be taken out of service at the beginning of December (followed by another ten at the start of January) over concerns with possible fractures in the steering column.

Route 48 was introduced as a replacement for trolleybus route 569, a Mon-Fri peak hour and Sunday morning route between North Woolwich and Aldgate, but with an added service all day Mon-Fri from Aldgate to Waterloo and a supplementary shuttle service between Waterloo and St Paul's. To serve workers, it had a very limited weekend service over the former trolleybus route, with morning and lunchtime journeys only on Saturday and five morning journeys on Sundays. It lasted just over five years, being cut back to Aldgate in the meantime at the time of stage 12 in November 1961. RM 94 is seen about to enter Aldwych.

Six months after they arrived at Poplar, from May 1960, the garage began to use spare RMs on Saturday and Sunday on the Isle of Dogs route 56. This allocation became Saturday only five months later and ceased altogether in May 1961 when the Poplar allocation reverted to RTL. RM 22 is seen in Millwall with a wartime bomb-damaged dock landscape and rows of early post-war prefabs.

Poplar garage received an allocation on route 23 with stage 4 of the trolleybus conversion and its share was worked with RMs, while Barking's larger share continued with RTs. The route had paralleled the 567/665 over the section between Barking and Aldgate and so was given this part to play in their replacement. RM 96 is seen in Poplar.

On Sundays Poplar used RMs on route 9, which ran over the Barking to Aldgate section of the 23 on this day as part of a very long Sunday version of the route between Becontree Heath and Mortlake. A driver who worked this duty told me that it was not unusual for crews to forget the right bus stops that applied in the central area when working the full length from the east London garages. Like the 23, the 9 continued with RTs from Barking on Sundays. RM 97 is seen in Kensington High Street.

Stage five in February 1960 was more straightforward than stage four in having fewer changes to the existing route patterns. It gave West Ham a second allocation of RMs and Walthamstow a first. Route 58 was a direct replacement of trolleybus 685 and route 69 directly replaced the 669. RMs 18 and 176 are both seen in Crownfield Road, Leyton, and RM 54 at North Woolwich, the latter once a busy trolleybus terminus in rush hours and completely transformed today. Many of the problems with the RMs in stage four were experienced at stage five also (and indeed stage six) and there were major programmes in progress in connection with rectification or replacement of some major components.

Route 25 had some special workings to the very large Ford car plant at Dagenham. RMs were available at the times they were needed and so they were used. They were not shown in the route allocation books even though blind displays for this working were on West Ham blinds. According to an observer who lived in the area at the time, they worked in service on the 25 from/to Becontree Heath and he saw the odd one working through Ilford to and from West Ham garage. The intermediate blinds were not changed and the drivers took advantage of this to speed back home and ignore as many bus stops as possible.

Trolleybus routes 689 and 690 had a loop operation between Upton Park and East Ham. In replacement, two new RM routes were introduced: 162 and 272. The 162 also replaced part of bus route 62, which no doubt influenced the choice of route number. It ran between Little Heath and Stratford via Barking, being extended from Little Heath to Mayesbrook Park in October 1961. The 272 was a shorter service between Stratford and East Ham, though with an extension to the Royal Albert Docks in Monday to Friday peak hours (or in the terminology of the time 'rush hours'). RM 26 is seen at Mayesbrook Park, RMs 23 and 60 are seen at the junction of Plashet Road and Stopford Road, also known as Upton Cross, and RM 61 is at Stratford Broadway. Both routes were operated with RMs from West Ham. Barking had a share of route 162 with RTs. In converting trolleybus routes to RM operation, the original expectation that more buses than trolleybuses might be needed to compensate for the reduced number of seats per vehicle was very often reversed. Sometimes large reductions were made in the number of buses allocated at the time of conversion compared with the number of trolleybuses. Routes 689 and 690, as examples, had an allocation of 26 trolleybuses immediately prior to their withdrawal, whereas the new replacement routes had 20 buses – and four of these were the RTs from Barking for the partial replacement of route 62. Part of the savings came from scheduling efficiencies but frequency reductions were also made.

Route 257 took over from trolleybus 557 and received an extension from Liverpool Street to London Bridge in Monday to Friday rush hours. Two RMs are seen on the forecourt of Walthamstow garage on the first day, 3rd February 1960, and RM 243 is in Bishopsgate at the Liverpool Street starting point of the route. Walthamstow was included in both stages five and six, so had a double dose of problems with new vehicles. West Ham which had featured in stage four, now had a role in stage five and would also at stage six, by which time much had been achieved (at not inconsiderable expense) in sorting out the problems.

The trolleybus was of course the Routemaster's main reason for existence. It had also given London Transport its first experience with integral construction when some chassisless trolleybuses were built in the years between 1936 and 1939. Chassisless trolleybus 1441 is about to pass stationary RM 149 new into service on route 256, a completely new service introduced between Moorgate and Chingford Mount covering much of the old 557 as far as Leyton and then the northern part of the 685 between there and Walthamstow. It also served new roads between Hackney and Clapton Stadium and deviated from the 257 at Shoreditch to run to Moorgate, Finsbury Square, the location of this view.

At the sixth stage in April 1960, revised route 41 and new route 278 replaced trolleybuses on route 687, splitting the service through Leyton into two. The 41 retained its Sunday RTs from Holloway and its daily RTWs from Tottenham, RMs allocated to West Ham being given a share of the route on Mondays to Saturdays. The 278 was an RM route from the start but it had some morning peak journeys worked by RTs/RTLs off route 25's allocation. This also applied to routes 58 and 69, and all three routes saw the older types substituting at other times when RMs were unavailable. The weekend service on the 278 was revised from January 1962 under the number 278A. RM 277 is seen after its first overhaul, when it had received this earlier body. With this stage the first RMs with opening front upper deck windows (254 on) and also the first with WLT marks entered service, with almost unbroken blocks of RMs from 220-248 and 254-310 being allocated for it between West Ham and Walthamstow garages, where they joined earlier RMs already in service including RMs 249, 250 and 253 at West Ham which had entered passenger service in March. The first of the WLT registered buses, RM 301, is seen at the Park Royal Vehicles factory earlier in April. The opening windows, at a cost of £18 10s per pair, had been decided on in the latter part of 1959 following complaints from some passengers and conductors about ventilation.

The old 623 trolleybus route had a terminus at Woodford (Napier Arms), shared with the 625, which was hardly a major traffic objective. It would probably not be unfair to describe it as being in the middle of nowhere. Serving a tree-lined stretch of road by which it was reached, it was a terminus inherited from tram days. With the introduction of RMs the opportunity was taken to divert the replacement 123 route at Woodford New Road to run to Ilford in place of route 41 as seen in this view at St Olaf's Church, Woodberry Down at Manor House. The bus is facing west with the bus being at the setting down point. The driver has already set the blind for the return journey. Stage six was a good example of how the new freedom to make major changes in routeings was used.

Route 275 took over from trolleybus route 625 (Woodford to Wood Green), the Monday to Friday service being extended from Woodford to Woodford Green at one end and from Wood Green to Enfield at the other. RMs like this one were plentiful in east London by now, and a major spread into north London was under way. RM 161 has turned at the old trolleybus terminus of Napier Arms mentioned in the caption above for the 123, where some scheduled journeys on the 275 continued to terminate.

One of the later bodies with non-opening windows, RM 249 is seen at Hornsey Rise Gardens. The 41 retained its Sunday RTs from Holloway and its daily RTWs from Tottenham at this time, RMs allocated to West Ham being given a share of the route on Mondays to Saturdays.

In May 1959 RM 6 had been the first production RM to be delivered for service to London Transport from Park Royal Vehicles, beating by a few days RMs 5 and 7. This view at Turnpike Lane shows the bus at its second garage, Walthamstow, which operated RMs on the 144 on Sundays only from May to October 1960 and then again from May 1963. Weekend RMs from Wood Green were added soon after. Tottenham's Saturday only operation was converted to RM in December 1962 following the introduction of RMs on the 73.

Some closely related trolleybus routes that in the Central bus department at that time would have had a single route number, with one of the variations distinguished by a suffix letter, had separate numbers as trolleybus services. New bus routes 249 and 249A were examples, these replacing the 697 and 699, which each had the same termini (Chingford Mount and Victoria & Albert Docks) but a variation in routeing at the southern end. This was another case where trolleybus route numbering reflected the practice from tram days and where Central bus policy took over. A 249B was added in October 1962, to serve the Yardley Lane Estate. The night service on route 699 was replaced by new night bus 299, renumbered N99 five months later when it was decided to make available further 200 series numbers available for trolleybus replacement routes. This was felt necessary following the summer 1960 decision to add the Fulwell routes to the conversion programme, though in the event fewer than a handful of the old night route numbers were needed. RM 203 is seen in Chingford. RM 34 has one of a small number of early RM bodies to have had its original front upper deck windows replaced with the winding design. This view is at the V&A Docks in October 1961. Low numbered RMs normally only received the winding windows at overhaul by getting a later body – or as part of accident repair damage. In 1963 two overhaul float bodies were built and these were used for RMs 90 and 162 at their first overhauls. Both bodies had the opening front windows.

Routes from Hammersmith depot were brought forward owing, Ken Blacker tells us in his London trolleybus history, to the wish to close Hammersmith depot without further delay. At stage seven in July 1960 the large garage at neighbouring Shepherd's Bush took on the new replacement services, affording worthwhile economies. The 220 was the main replacement for the 630, covering the whole of the old route but with an extension to Park Royal in peak hours. The regular northern terminus at the junction of Harrow Road and Scrubs Lane, for many years described as 'Near Willesden Junction' by 630 trolleybuses, was another terminus that fell short of a major traffic objective, but the opportunity was not taken to extend the 220 to Willesden Junction. RM 337 is seen in Scrubs Lane with Harrow Road in the background.

The 268 followed the route pattern of the peak hour only 626 but with an all-day service between Clapham Junction and Willesden Junction. The 626 and 628 shared the same route between Clapham Junction and Harlesden, where at the Jubilee Clock the 628 turned right to terminate at Craven Park and the 626 went via Willesden Junction towards Acton. There had been an intention at the planning stage to extend the 628 replacement route to Sudbury but this was dropped, enabling the 626 and 628 to be merged. This view in King Street, Acton, shows RM 333 on the peak hour extension from Willesden Junction to Acton Market Place.

An effect of the stage seven changes was the extension of route 64, a long established Croydon garage bus route between Addington or Selsdon and West Croydon. Under stage seven it was extended to Wimbledon Stadium via Mitcham and Tooting Broadway. It received a part allocation of RMs with a new share of the route given to Elmers End garage. This covered the southern part of the old 630 trolleybus route along with new route 220 and took over the 630 journeys to Wimbledon Stadium, a greyhound track always referred to as Summerstown in trolleybus days. RM 263 is seen in Mitcham Road, Tooting.

Stage seven also took in the trolleybus service that ran up Highgate Hill and was another interruption in the steady anticlockwise march of the RM around London from the east. Alone among Highgate depot's routes, the 611 was included at this stage to enable the withdrawal of the run-back brake equipped trolleybuses used on it. The route was directly replaced by the 271, a route that uniquely among former trolleybus services exists with the same two termini on Monday to Fridays 60 years after the conversion. The Jensen pantechnicon alongside was, like the RM, of integral and all-aluminium construction.

Before returning to its progressive path across north London, the conversion scheme next dealt with Hanwell depot's 607 and 655 routes in November 1960, enabling the removal of all wiring between Hammersmith and Clapham Junction and leaving Fulwell depot as the only one serving routes south of the Thames with trolleybuses. Two new RM services replaced the 607, the 207 being identical to the former trolleybus route. Hanwell was the first garage to operate RM 546, the first RM to go abroad on a promotion tour for Britain, and (later) the three production RMs (632, 870 and 1009) fitted with Leyland engines for assessment alongside AECs.

The 207A provided a supplementary service to the 207 between Southall and Shepherd's Bush. It also took over part of route 120 between Southall and Hayes Station and continued beyond Shepherd's Bush via the 49 route to Chelsea, thus providing some new links. RM 418 is seen at The Broadway, Hayes.

Route 255 was one of a few London bus routes that no-one would have wanted to travel from one end to the other, its main service running between Acton (Bromyard Avenue) and Hammersmith via Hanwell Broadway and Brentford, a route length about ten times the distance between its two termini. It was extended from Hammersmith to Clapham Junction in rush hours. At the time of its introduction it was the only RM route to pass London Transport's Chiswick works, which may possibly the reason the first Leyland RMs were allocated to Hanwell when Shepherd's Bush was closer to the works. On Saturday evenings and Sundays the route was considerably shortened to run between Hanwell and Brentford only.

Hanwell used five spare RMs on Sundays on route 97 and RM 544 is seen at West Ealing. This was one of only a few cases where spare weekend RMs were used on RT routes during the progress of the trolleybus programme. The buses ran alongside RTs from Southall garage.

With stage nine, at the beginning of February 1961, the march of the Routemaster resumed from where it had left off with the completion of stage six. Highgate and Stamford Hill received their first allocations of RMs, a major influx occurring at the former. Route 17 was the main replacement for the North Finchley to Holborn loop routes 517 and 617, but served the Grays Inn Road side of the loop only and was extended south to Camberwell Green on Mondays to Fridays. It was one of a number of new north-south links provided under the trolleybus to bus conversions. RM 732 is seen in Archway Road.

Route 63 was an established bus route that played a small part in trolleybus replacement by being extended from its northern terminus at King's Cross to Parliament Hill Fields. It was one of three routes, the others being the 39 and 45, extended to replace trolleybus routes 513 and 613 but was the only one of them to receive a daily RM allocation, albeit small. This was so that Highgate, which was given a minority share of the 63, could be a 100% RM. The night service on the 513/613 was replaced by new RM route N93 with an extension to Charing Cross via Fleet Street, at that time centre of national newspaper printing. In the second photo RM 606 is delivered to Highgate depot while trolleybus 1575 is about to start one of its last journeys in service.

Three new Routemaster services at stage nine directly took over trolleybus routes without change, these being the 214 (615), 239 (639) and 253 (653). All began life as tram routes. RM 421 passes under the railway bridge in Highgate Road, Kentish Town. Just visible on the nearside wing is the width gauge fitted to a number of RMs at this time to aid the driver when drawing into the kerb, not visible from the cab. The Unzipp a Banana advert among the posters was in the same league as Drinka Pinta Milka Day and Go to Work on an Egg for slogans that everyone was very familiar with during this period. All three were to be seen on placards like this, in newspapers and on television where an Unzipp a Banana song could be heard. Why the first word was spelt with two Ps is unknown (no answers on a postcard please).

These views show the other two routes introduced at stage nine that were unchanged from the trolleybus routes. The Finsbury Square terminus, once humming with trolleybuses, by now had more RM routes terminating there than trolleybus ones, with just routes 609 and 641 continuing to serve it until November. RM 597 is nearing this southern terminus of the route in travelling along City Road.

The 253 was a very busy horseshoe shaped route between Tottenham Court Road and Aldgate via Stamford Hill and no-one would have travelled the whole route to reach one or other of the termini. Only in relatively recent times has the service been split into two routes. It had a substantial service requirement of 52 RMs and initially operated from Highgate garage. With the next stage, twelve weeks later, the allocation was split between Highgate and Edmonton when the latter received its first RMs. Highgate's RM 1005 is seen in Finsbury Park.

Route 45 received a small and very short-lived Sunday allocation of three RMs from Highgate garage with stage nine as part of providing replacement services for the 513 and 613 trolleybus routes. The route was extended daily from Farringdon Street to Hampstead Heath. The RM allocation lasted 12 Sundays from 5th February 1961 to 22nd April, after which the three-bus Sunday share of the route moved to Chalk Farm with RTWs. The route received RMs on a daily basis from January 1966 using secondhand vehicles. RM 514 is seen at South Kensington.

Route 143 was another of the existing bus routes to be extended, this time from Archway Station to Farringdon Street. The route moved into Highgate garage and was fully worked by RMs from this time. It served the Farringdon Street side of the Holborn loop used by trolleybuses.

Stage ten took place on 26th April 1961 and involved Edmonton, Highgate, Tottenham and Wood Green garages. Like many trolleybus routes, the 627 stopped short of a major traffic objective and was one of a number that had to turn off and pick up passengers near the Euston Road end of Tottenham Court Road. Hopes by the LPTB of getting further into central London with a terminus at Bedford Square or even Trafalgar Square generated insurmountable objections. The resulting long route from Waltham Cross to Victoria was operated in two overlapping sections: Waltham Cross to Tottenham Court Road (Mondays to Saturdays only and matching the old 627) and Edmonton to Victoria Station (daily). RM 760 at Finsbury Park displays *This is the New Routemaster* above the front lower deck passenger window.

No southward extension was made to the 269, which simply replaced the 629 without alteration and continued to terminate in Maple Street, three years before the Post Office Tower was opened there. From 26th April 1961 until 7th November 1961 the 269 had a Monday to Friday allocation of five RMs from West Green in that garage's latter days. Both the 127 and 629 were affected in a small way by the one-way system introduced for Tottenham Court Road on 1st May 1961, five days after their introduction; indeed the 629 conversion was brought forward in connection with this. Southbound traffic was diverted to run via Gower Street, the 127 travelling the length of it and the 269 using the top end only. Both this bus and the 127 opposite carry further examples of London Transport's attempts to attract advertisers.

The 659 was another trolleybus route to use the Holborn loop and two new routes were envisaged to replace it, a 258 running via the Farringdon Road side of the loop and then on to Clapham Junction and the 259 running via Grays Inn Road to end at the established 659 terminus in Charterhouse Street. In the event only the 259 was introduced; it was the lowest new route number not previously used by London Transport, a distinction that would have applied to the 258 had that been used. In this splendid summer's day view at Finsbury Park the conductor of RM 662 stands on the edge of the platform of what seems like an empty bus, presumably following close after another southbound journey, and followed by two other new RMs. Both this and the RM behind have all the winding windows and the bonnet number plate flap open so the day must have been a very hot one. The 259 is passing north London's Majestic Ballroom, a former cinema dating from 1909 that fifty years later became a venue that catered for dancing, concerts, wrestling and bingo – the last named having taken off in Britain in the late 1950s and probably at its peak in the Sixties. Within two years of this view the venue also hosted concerts starring Merseybeat pop groups including The Beatles and Gerry and the Pacemakers. Its transport connection is that it stood on the site of a horse tram depot that closed in the first few years of the 20th Century. Its horse-drawn trams ran between Finsbury Park and Moorgate via two different routes.

The 276 (Tottenham – Finsbury Park – Camden Town – Oxford Circus – Trafalgar Square – Vauxhall – Brixton) was a new north-south route that covered part of the 127 and opened new connections. With 276 being an anagram of 627, this probably influenced the choice. The new connections the route gave did not prove to have a great demand and the route consequently had a short life. Eighteen months after its introduction its limited Saturday service (terminating at Trafalgar Square from the north) was withdrawn and the Monday to Friday service followed under a year later in August 1963. RM 397 is seen at Thane Villas, Finsbury Park.

One of the new buses sent to Highgate garage later in the year was the experimental unpainted RM 664, received into stock seven months after RMs 663 and 665 and placed into service in July 1961. Principally intended for the 276, it also appeared on the 127 at weekends. Highgate was not one of the better garages when it came to looking after the appearance of its buses and by the end of its time there is was looking fairly uncared for. It moved in December 1961 to route 23 at Poplar for a month before going to Rye Lane. This view is in Streatham Hill opposite Brixton garage.

On 28th September 1960, Durrant had asked a senior member of his staff to obtain information on the likely cost of modifying 24 production RMs to 30ft length by the insertion of a shorter bay between the front and rear halves. The RMLs were the result and were built at the Park Royal Vehicles factory in summer 1961; at first classified ER (applied to 880-883) but changed to RML on 30th August in association with the reclassification of Leyland prototype RML 3 to RM 3. This posed official view of RML 898 in July 1962 shows 276 blinds, although RMLs never worked on this route nor at this time from Highgate garage. It was not until May 1964, almost three years after delivery, that this bus entered service at Finchley. It was out of use (apart from training duties) until selected for a transatlantic journey to San Francisco for a London Week there from 12th to 17th November 1962. After this it remained in store until a second American visit the following August.

Trolleybus route 609 was partly converted to RM on Sundays from 30th April 1961 as part of stage ten and the trolleybus route number was kept until the Monday to Saturday service followed suit in November 1961 as part of stage twelve. Only ten of Highgate's RMs are believed to have received blinds for the 609, which required five RMs running alongside Finchley trolleybuses. RM 586 is seen in Islington and RM 587 is seen leaving Finsbury Square. The Routemaster corner (target) poster was fairly common at the time. Stage ten required total scheduled allocations of 144 RMs, more vehicles than at any other stage. Highgate became the largest operator of Routemasters and remained so throughout the rest of the programme.

The 279 was another one of the conversions of a trolleybus route that was straightforward, in this case replacing the 679 from Smithfield to Waltham Cross, where RM 725 is seen. In addition a new Monday to Friday route, numbered 279A, ran from Tottenham Hale to Flamstead End and on Saturdays the 279 was extended to the latter point with the Flamstead End buses starting at Tottenham. RM 720 is seen at the Tottenham Hale end of the route.

With stage 11 on 19th July 1961, the replacement of trolleybuses by Routemasters was now under a year away from completion. The 67 took over the Monday to Saturday service of route 647 and was extended from Stamford Hill, where the trolleybuses used to do a U-turn in the main road, to Northumberland Park. RM 783 is seen in Tottenham Green.

Opposite top: Routes 243 and 243A, as well as 67, were operated from Stamford Hill, which shared the 149 with Edmonton. The 243 replaced Holborn loop routes 543 and 643, with the new service running one way round the loop – via Grays Inn Road like the majority of Holborn loop replacement routes. The new N83 took over the night journeys on the 543/643. Services on night routes at this time were very limited, but the N83 was one that ran daily, albeit with only five round trips with one extra on Sunday mornings. The route had an extension, parallel with the N93, south from Holborn via Fleet Street and Strand to Charing Cross. RM 860 is seen at Stamford Hill.

Opposite bottom: The 243A was a Sunday only route that partly replaced the Sunday service on route 647 and the Sunday only route 649A. It followed the route of the old 647 and the new Mon-Sat route 67 between Shoreditch High Street and London Docks, Liverpool Street losing the service that had been provided by the 649A. This, however, was maintained by the new 149. Two 243As are seen in this view at St Peter's Way, Dalston. The frequency between 10am and 3pm was at its peak of 4-5 minutes.

On Mondays to Fridays the new 149 operated in two overlapping sections, the first of which – between Waltham Cross to Liverpool Street – was a direct replacement for trolleybus route 649. RM 751 is seen in Queen Street in the City. The other section of the route – in effect a new route despite sharing the same number – ran between Stamford Hill and Liverpool Street and then continued via Bank, Southwark Bridge, Waterloo, Lambeth Bridge and Horseferry Road to Victoria. At weekends and on Monday to Friday evenings the first only of these sections operated.

Night route N83 was introduced in replacement of night journeys on trolleybus routes 543 and 643 with an extension from Holborn to Charing Cross. It was one of four night services at the time that needed just one bus to operate it and here soon after midnight on 19th July 1961 RM 860 is about to set off from Stamford Hill on its first journey. London Transport's own staff were among those who used these services and one member of staff from Stamford Hill has taken a front seat for his journey home.

The twelfth stage saw the introduction of the first 30ft long Routemasters (RMLs) and the first use on Routemasters of upper and lower case via blinds. Comparisons at Chiswick in the summer of 1960 between via blinds using all upper case lettering and mock-ups using upper and lower case for the via blinds had been inconclusive but it was decided to change to the latter on aesthetic grounds. It was felt by some that the new via blinds would also give greater prominence to the ultimate destination blind. With the conversion of the 609, the brief Sunday operation of RMs alongside trolleybuses on the route came to an end with its daily replacement being numbered 104. The introduction of RMLs needed to be negotiated with the busman's union, who agreed to their introduction after London Transport offered an average reduction of duty time of 5% for crews when working on the 72-seaters. It was agreed that RMLs would not be used on Sundays. RMLs 880-880-894 entered service at the time of the conversion, 895-897 in December and 899 in January. The others were initially placed in store or used for overseas tours. A scheduled Monday to Friday allocation of 26 trolleybuses was replaced by 19 buses, with substantial peak-hour frequency reductions as was often the case elsewhere. This could hardly have endeared the Routemaster to those affected.

The 221 took over from the 521/621 but serving only the Farringdon Road side of the Holborn loop before terminating in Stonecutter Street. The Grays Inn Road side was covered by other trolleybus replacement services already in place and by an extension of route 168 from Farringdon Street to Turnpike Lane. The 221 had a number of allocation changes in its first six months. Finchley worked it daily, but Wood Green had a minority Saturday allocation from the route's introduction in November 1961 until January 1962 (at stage 13) and an allocation of seven RMs on Sundays from May alongside six RMs from Finchley. The 168 was in effect a version of the 258 mentioned under route 259. RM 912 is seen at North Finchley.

The 141 was another route, like the 149, introduced in two sections one of which was a straight replacement of a trolleybus service, in this case the 641. RM 823 is seen on this in Green Lanes. The second section was a replacement for route bus route 179 (Grove Park to Farringdon Street) but was renumbered 141 in view of its lengthy extension over part of that route from Ludgate Circus to Turnpike Lane. No buses ran all the way from Winchmore Hill to Grove Park. The 141 was the first service to operate along the new London Wall, with its sleek new high-rise office blocks neighbouring the Barbican residential development and RM 953 is seen half way along it. A 141A weekend-only variant took a different route north of central London to terminate at Finsbury Park. This and the 141's southern section were operated from New Cross, giving that garage its first Routemasters. Other garages involved with stage 12 were Finchley, Wood Green and Highgate.

The first week of 1962 brought freezing conditions, snow and stage 13 of trolleybus replacement. At this stage the first RMs numbered above 1000 entered service. RM 1064 is seen at the Sudbury end of the former 662 with a Stonebridge trolleybus blind fending off some of the bitterly cold air from the radiator. The merging of route 18 into the old trolleybus route was a fairly late change to plans that had envisaged a 262 taking over. The 18 became a route operated in three sections: the existing Edgware to Wembley Empire Pool service, which retained RTs until 1964, an extended service from Paddington Green beyond Sudbury to Edgware via Harrow, and a service from Sudbury to London Bridge which absorbed route 18B.

Opposite: The 293 would have been numbered 262A if the 662 had been directly replaced by the 262, as originally planned. This Monday to Friday peak hour route from Paddington Green to Acton via Harlesden, unnumbered in trolleybus days, gave a morning and evening service to a route that had been morning peak only in trolleybus days. RM 1035 is seen in Harlesden.

The buses used for stage 13 included a number of second hand RMs from Poplar and West Ham. This view shows a number of buses at Craven Park on transfer to Stonebridge for service from there, including RM 177 from West Ham. RM 177 had been taken out of service in November 1960 and did nothing for a year, being stored in Walthamstow garage until it moved to West Ham as a trainer in November 1961.

The 645 was a U-shaped route from Barnet via Cricklewood to a roundabout north of Edgware. Its replacement, the 245, was cut back to North Finchley and extended down the road at the other end to Stanmore Station, where a passenger is seen stepping off Cricklewood's RM 1046.

The section of route between North Finchley and Barnet was taken over by new route 260, whose main function was to replace the 660 trolleybus between North Finchley and Hammersmith. It was another route operated in sections, with no buses running the full route from Barnet to Hammersmith. The number 260 was the first case of a route number's second use on an RM, the former 260 (renumbered 60 in October 1961 so 260 would be available) having been worked by RM 1 during its second period of passenger service from Cricklewood.

The 266 was a straight replacement of trolleybus route 666, running between Edgware and Hammersmith, which until 1956 had been a peak hour only route but then became all day on Monday to Friday only. For the last three years of its life it was a daily route and 266 followed suit. Twenty RMs were scheduled from Stonebridge and eight from Cricklewood. RM 253, the last built with full front windows, is at Acton Vale and was transferred from West Ham via a short spell of training work from Shepherd's Bush.

Opposite top: Overnight on 8th/9th May 1962 RMs replaced the last of the trolleybus fleet. The 281 was a direct replacement for the 601 (Tolworth to Twickenham) with a small extension at the latter from King Street to the railway station. RM 1119 is seen below the overhead wiring in King Street where the 601 trolleybuses used to turn. The 281 was allocated to Fulwell together with the 267 and 285.

Opposite bottom: Trolleybus routes 602 and 603 had a loop working in Kingston, the former working it anticlockwise and the latter working clockwise. New routes 282 (daily) and 283 (Mon-Sat) were direct replacements for the 602 and 603 and maintained this pattern of operation. RMs 1071 and 1183 are seen in Surbiton.

Above: The service provided by the 605 trolleybus received a major extension when converted to bus operation. New RM route 285 was projected beyond the Teddington terminus of the 605 to run to London (Heathrow) Airport Central via Hampton Hill, Hanworth and Feltham. It was also extended at the other end from Wimbledon to Haydons Road station on Mondays to Saturdays. RM 1089 is seen at New Malden.

The service provided by the 657 was another to have an extension on conversion to bus operation. The Monday to Saturday replacement was provided by a long extension of route 117 (Egham to Hounslow) to Shepherd's Bush, though it was only on Saturdays that buses ran the full length, with the service operating in overlapping sections on Mondays to Fridays. RM 1055 is seen travelling in Goldhawk Road to the original 117 terminus at Egham while RM 1096 at the Shepherd's Bush end is working a duty that matches the old 657 route. The extended 117 had a scheduled requirement of 36 RMs, all allocated to Hounslow garage.

On Sundays the former 657 was covered by an extension of route 81B (London Airport to Hounslow) to Shepherd's Bush, which used RMs on this day. The Sunday service on route 81 was also converted to RM in December of the same year when Hounslow received further RMs for its small share of the major trunk route 73. From 12th June 1963, the daily conversion of this route the 81B took place using minority allocations of AEC engined RMs transferred from Cricklewood and Rye Lane, where new Leyland engined RMs replaced them.

Trolleybus route 604 covered the same roads as the 131 between Hampton Court and Kingston, so the opportunity was taken to extend the 131 to Wimbledon to replace it. The full route now ran from Walton to Wimbledon with a journey time of just under an hour, somewhat quicker than it would take today. RM 313, two years old when transferred into Norbiton for the conversion, is seen at East Molesey. It began its working life at Shepherds Bush.

Norbiton garage also took on the 282 and 283 routes, short services linking Kingston with The Dittons and Tolworth respectively. Each had a Monday to Friday allocation of just four buses.

Three RMs at Fulwell garage are seen on three of the new routes that saw the end of electric public transport in London streets until the introduction of trams in Croydon in the year 2000. Remains from tram days in south west London are in evidence. With the great expansion of one-way traffic schemes in the 1960s, the flexibility argument was a reasonable one at a time when the idea of contra-flow bus lanes was some way in the future. Concerns over diesel pollution were dismissed though.

One other small change affecting RMs that occurred with the revisions of 9th May 1962 was the introduction in east London of route 5B, a variation of route 5 that initially ran on Sundays only but from August ran on Saturdays also. Route 5 was withdrawn accordingly on these days. RM 89 is seen in Canning Town Station on a short working to Clerkenwell Green. The bus was one of those used for the service trials prior to the start of trolleybus replacement when it had a short period at Turnham Green on routes 91 and 27 in October and November 1959.

With trolleybus replacement completed, attention turned to the Green Line fleet, where the Routemaster Coach was seen as a means of reducing the number of vehicles needed for some of the services. The argument was that the almost 50% higher capacity of the RMC (57 seats compared with 39 in the Green Line RF) would enable the same number of seats per hour with fewer coaches. This was found to be a false economy as passengers were lost through the reduced frequencies. The RMCs, in their way, therefore contributed to the continuing decline of Green Line services through the rest of the 1960s. The first of the 1453-1520 batch of RMCs entered service on routes 715 and 715A on 29th August 1962 and the first of them is seen at Guildford. The other routes to receive RMCs when new were the 718, 720, 720A, 719, 716 and 716A and the programme was completed with these last two routes on 2nd January 1963. The last RMC delivery had been made from Park Royal a few days before Christmas. The arrangement by which the passenger doors opened and closed was a poor design and there were many instances of door failure. Laurie Akehurst recalls seeing one arrive at Harlow Bus Station with the conductor opening the emergency door to allow passengers to board and alight. The vehicles were capable of high speeds on clear runs like the one shown opposite in Harlow Road, Sawbridgeworth, and up to 60mph was recorded in places.

Planning for the replacement of RTs by Routemasters had reached a significant stage in August 1961 when London Transport sought authority from the British Transport Commission for the purchase of 1340 Routemasters to replace 1488 RT buses. These figures represented a 10% reduction in buses being achieved by way of reduced schedules to account for the additional seats on a Routemaster, a 14% increase in capacity for an RM compared with the RT and 28.5% in the case of RMLs, the first of which were being delivered at that time. The order was for delivery between 1963 and 1967 and followed on from the original order for 1520 that was in progress at the time, which when ordered had been the expected requirement for trolleybus replacement and a batch of coach Routemasters. The 1340 order was subsequently reduced by 100.

In November 1961 London Transport, during negotiations with the operating staff's union, made clear it wanted to link pay increases to the increased productivity that the RM could provide. The latter half of the 1950s and the first half of the 1960s comprised a period of difficult industrial relations as London Transport responded to a falling demand for bus services. The solution to persistent difficulties in recruiting enough operating staff was seen by LT as a reduction in the number of staff required. The solution from the point of view of the unions was seen as increasing pay. This was the background to the forthcoming replacement of RT family vehicles with Routemasters. It led to a stand-off that was to last twelve months.

By July 1962 the Central Bus Department decided that at the start of the 1962 winter programme on 10th October, RMs would replace RTs on a 9 for 10 basis on three routes centred on Harrow, these being 114, 140 and 158. This was seen as the first of a number of similar area-based schemes in parts of London where staff recruitment was difficult.

The union was notified of this intention in a letter dated 15th August 1962, by which time Harrow Weald garage destination blinds had been produced in readiness. The union was then advised that the 73 would be the next route after those at HD. On 20th August the union stated that the allocation of RMs to this route was also dependent 'to a certain degree' on the outcome of 'broader issues'. On 12th September the union further stated at a meeting chaired by Central Bus Operating Manager Fred Lloyd that unless an agreement was reached, staff would not operate RMs on routes 114, 140 and 158. The memo from the meeting tactfully records that 'Mr Lloyd noted these remarks and there followed a full exchange of views'. London Transport then announced that the conversion would take place on 24th October, which resulted in a strike at the two garages on Saturday 13th October and continuing resistance to the reduction in schedules. The conversion set for 24th October was postponed six days beforehand.

No agreement was reached and the planned conversion of routes at these two garages was abandoned on 6th November. Edgware would have lost three double deckers under the new schedules for the three routes combined and Harrow Weald four. The same schedule revisions did however see a 10% reduction in Edgware's single deck allocation, where nine RFs were now scheduled to replace ten TDs on route 240A. This reduction did take place, apparently without resistance. Destination blinds for the RM conversions of routes 114, 140 and 158 (those for Edgware having 140 displays only) that had been ordered in August and supplied to the garages in readiness then went to waste. All of the RMs that had been scheduled to go to Edgware entered service instead from Hendon on route 13 in January and the RMs that had been intended for Harrow Weald were shared between Hendon, Cricklewood, Rye Lane and Mortlake in December and January. RMs 1175/76/79/82/92/93, 1229/46/48/49/50/51/52/53 had been intended for Edgware and 1155/56/57/71/72/73/80/88/89/91/94, 1255/57/64/71/79 for Harrow Weald, HD's being a mix of AEC and Leyland vehicles. On 1st August, John Gascoine noted two of those intended for Edgware, RMs 1246 and 1249, stored ready in Cricklewood garage. The illustrated unused RM side blind for Harrow Weald was produced on 13th August.

114 Eastcote La. Harrow
Wealdstone High St
Harrow Weald
Stanmore Canons Pk

140 Burnt Oak Stn
Queensbury Kenton
Harrow Northolt
Yeading Hayes

158 Bushey Heath
Harrow Weald
Wealdstone Harrow
Eastcote Lane

After a backlog of new RMs had built up following the failure to reach agreement on reduced schedules, in November it was decided to start with two routes, 37 and 73, that needed large numbers of buses. Blinds for these were ordered from Aldenham on 23rd and 24th November and it must have been a major job to get them all ready by Wednesday 12th December, the date set for both routes. In fact a small start was made the previous Wednesday when the six-bus share of route 73 operated by Hounslow garage went over to RM using second-hand vehicles. Hounslow's RM 1072 is seen in Richmond. Not all of the 49 Tottenham workings on the morning of 12th December began with RMs, some of the new buses taking over from RTLs during the course of the day. John Gascoine tells us he was photographing first day RMs at Stoke

Newington Common and this photo shows RM 1301 after a mechanic from Tottenham garage had driven it there to sub for an RTL. The newly fitted blind had not yet been set to a route 73 destination and the platform strap had been in place to prevent passengers boarding. Hounslow garage had an existing RM allocation from stage 14 of the trolleybus conversion. Mortlake used its RMs on route 9 on Sundays, when there were sufficient spare from its 73 allocation, and it was not long before the route received RMs daily. The RMs ran alongside Poplar's Sunday RMs on the route. Tottenham's night route N90 was also converted.

Back in 1940, the 37 from Chelverton Road garage had been one of the first routes to receive RTs to replace older vehicles. Now it was one of the first to get new RMs in replacement of RTLs. On 12th December this was converted with the scheduling of 21 RMs to Stockwell and 14 to Putney. All of these allocations were on a one-for-one basis in replacement of RTLs, but RTLs remained for a time on Stockwell's operation on Saturdays (much larger than its Monday to Friday allocation) and on Rye Lane's Sunday only share of the route. The latter was mostly converted to RM when Monday to Saturday route 13 received RMs five days later and fully converted when the 36B received RMs the following January. Stockwell's Saturday RTLs remained for a few more years. These two views were taken in Brixton in summer 1963.

Less than a week after the 37 and 73 conversions used up a large number of what had been a growing number of new RMs waiting unlicensed to be deployed, route 13 from Hendon and Rye Lane was changed over on Monday 17th. Spare RMs on Sundays were used on routes 113, 240 and 260, the last having been RT from Hendon on this day since introduction a year before. The new buses replaced RTs and, as part of its allocation, all of the RMs that had originally been earmarked for Edgware's share of route 140 went to Hendon. Two of those, RMs 1246 and 1229, are seen in these views at Hendon garage and a wintery Mill Hill village.

The last of what had become something of a stockpile of new RMs was used up on Christmas Eve 1962, one week after the conversion of the 13. Most of the allocation on route 16 was converted from RT on this date and the rest followed on 1st January 1963. RM 1691, allocated to Cricklewood later that year, is seen at Hyde Park Corner. The first examples of the main batches of Leyland engined RMs entered service with this conversion alongside eight AEC engined initially. Also converted with the 16 was Cricklewood's N94.

The major trunk routes that made up the 36 group were next in line for RMs, a conversion that required around 100 buses for a scheduled requirement of 89. The routes were shared between neighbouring garages Peckham and Rye Lane. The latter's share was converted first, with RMs appearing on routes 36A and 36B from mid-January. Britain was in the midst of a very cold winter at the time – the third coldest on record – and bitter snow showers were coming in on cold winds from Scandinavia. RM 664 on its first day of service at Rye Lane (28th January 1963) is seen with some of the effects, an appearance perhaps acquired during its transfer from Poplar. It was hardly a good advert for the new buses on the route. The completion of all three services occurred on 1st April.

Together with the conversion of the 36 group, route 173 (Nunhead Circular) was converted to RM on Saturdays and Sundays and night routes N85 and N86 were also converted. Later in the same year, routes 78 (on Sundays) and 188 (on Saturdays) followed. RM 1659 is seen at Peckham Rye and RM 306 in Bermondsey. Later in life, RM 1659 was severely damaged by fire at Peckham garage in April 1972.

In the spring of 1962 RMs had begun to be used on London Transport's Round London Sightseeing Tour, taking over from RTs, which had operated it since introduction of the service as part of a range of excursions in Festival of Britain year 1951. It was still listed in the official allocation book as 'Excursion No.1'. For 1963 new vehicles RMs 1524, 1533 and 1563 were allocated to New Cross garage for a service requirement of two buses and these were normally kept separate from normal service buses as they had public address equipment fitted for use by the guide/conductor. RM 1668, seen at Eccleston Bridge in Victoria, replaced RM 1563 in August.

In February 1963 RM 1414 was loaned to Manchester Corporation for a couple of weeks. It ran from Parrs Wood garage on the busy 41/42 Wilmslow Road services alongside Leyland PD2s. It is seen at the terminus of the 42 at Didsbury Library. Passengers and conductors liked its interior finish and smooth ride, and drivers were impressed by the power steering, automatic gearbox and lively performance. RM 1414 was able to show the latter when it ran for a few days on the Wilmslow Road 162/162 limited stop service to Gatley. Below, RM 1414 is seen inward bound on the 162 service at the stop outside the Manchester University Students' Union. A notice in the front bulkhead window read 'This is a London Transport Routemaster on loan to Manchester Corporation'. It was not the first time that Manchester had borrowed a London bus – it had RT 19 on loan in 1941. RM 1414 may have impressed but there was little real chance that the Corporation would buy any. The Transport Department was at the fore of operators pressing for one-man operation of double deckers and the next double-deck order was for 30 Fleetlines and 72 Atlanteans.

On conversion of route 9 from RTL, Mortlake became the first garage previously operated entirely by RT family buses to be converted to all-RM. The changeover of that garage's share of the route between the first week of April and mid-May 1963 followed Mortlake's other former RTL route, the 73, which had received RMs four months earlier. The route was shared with Dalston garage, where the new vehicles took over from RTLs (RTWs on Saturdays). By now there were seven garages with a 100% Routemaster allocation. As with the photo of route 16 earlier, the photographer has made a point of getting the Park Lane Hilton in the background. This impressive piece of architecture by Emanuel Gran caused quite a stir at the time and stands today as one of the finest buildings from a mediocre period. Its 30 storeys were the maximum that the London County Council would allow.

The 253A was a summer Sunday only variation of the 253 introduced in May 1963 and designed to give a direct link from places on the 253 to London Zoo. It had been intended to introduce this route as part of stage nine of the trolleybus scheme, when the 253 started. It ran for one season only with this number, returning for summer 1964 as the 253B but otherwise without change. Between the two summers a new 253A had been introduced, operated by RTLs. RM 508 is seen in Amhurst Park.

The conversion of Muswell Hill's Monday to Saturday 43 route on 21st June 1963, with a scheduled requirement of 30 buses, enabled the complete conversion of the Sunday services on all of its daily double-deck routes. Hence, on that day of the week routes 102, 134, 134A and 212 received RMs. The services included the summer Sunday extension of route 102 to High Beach. Routes 134 and 134A became RM daily from the garage in July 1964.

Route 63 had received a small minority allocation of RMs from Highgate garage as part of the trolleybus replacement. The much larger share operated by Peckham remained RT until July 1963, when that too was taken over by RMs from the 17th of the month, hence the route's appearance twice in this book. Between the first and second stages of its change to RM, via blinds had changed from being all upper case to upper and lower case. From October 1963 a 63A was introduced, running on Saturdays and Sundays in place of the 63 and 239 on these days.Later in life, RM 1368 was converted to a single-deck Chiswick experimental department engineers' vehicle following fire damage to the upper deck in 1973. The vehicle is now in preservation.

The withdrawal of route 276 after service on 13th August 1963 released fifteen RMs and these were used to convert routes 85 and 85A the following day. Putney was the operating garage and it already had an allocation of RMs for its share of the 37; the conversion of the 85/A doubled its RM fleet. RM 1586 is seen at the Roehampton end of the 85A.

The next conversion reverted to the use of brand new RMs, as appropriate for a major route like the 14, and gave further RMs to Putney. Spare RMs on Sundays were used on route 74, a route that was later converted to RM in November/December 1965 but using secondhand RMs from the conversion of route 24 (which was the next to receive RMs) from RM to XA operation. RM 1000 had unique registration letters and was a temporary break from registrations including the letters LT. Originally allocated to West Ham garage in March 1962, the bus moved to Cricklewood garage in January 1963 and then to Putney in October for this conversion.

The first RMs with the absence of an offside route number blind, a plain panel taking its place, entered service during the conversion of route 24. The first RM not to be so equipped was 1743 and earlier vehicles very quickly had the offside blind glass painted red, as seen here on RM 1729. RMs lasted two years on the route, as the 24 was among the services on which front entrance XAs were trialled following a new union agreement on pay and conditions. RMLs took over subsequently, initially to provide comparison with the Atlanteans.

Route 7 was the last conversion to RM of 1963. Operated by Middle Row garage, RMs from the route's allocation that were spare on Sundays were used on route 28. Among the RMs to enter service at the garage in December 1963 was RM 1768, the first RM to suffer a disastrous fire. Here it is seen in Cambridge Gardens, Ladbroke Grove, not long after entering service. The spectacular fire that destroyed it occurred at Marble Arch in July 1966. The bus had been taken out of service before its fire and was on its way back to Middle Row garage.

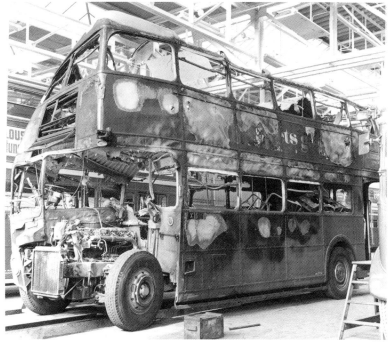

RM 1768 is seen at Marble Arch after the fire brigade had put out its fire, which took hold quite quickly after the driver and conductor (the only two people on the bus at the time) had moved to a safe place on the edge of Hyde Park. The wreck was taken to Chiswick, where the other photos were taken, for a thorough inspection which resulted in the finding that the cause was oil being ignited by an overheated flywheel.

These views show further the extent of the fire damage. Soon after the incident, an emergency programme was undertaken of fitting a fusible plug to the flywheel that would melt before the flywheel oil temperature reached a combustible level. The number RM 1768 was to reappear in May 1967 with body B294, reducing the float by one.

Route 6B was a new Saturday only route from 29 January 1964, introduced to replace route 6 and part of route 257 on that day of the week and running between Kensal Rise and Chingford. It was introduced with RMs from Walthamstow (from the 257 allocation) and RTWs from Willesden (from the 6). The RTW allocation on the route remained until the 6 began to receive RMs in 1965. RM 161 operating from Willesden rounds Marble Arch.

The 256A began on the same day as the 6B, also on Saturdays only, as part of the same package of changes to replace the 257 on the section not covered by the 6B. It was one of a number of former trolleybus services tinkered with within a few years of the changeover. RM 140 had been one of Walthamstow's original allocation of Routemasters in February 1960, though it had spent a period at West Ham between then and the time of this photo taken in Powerscroft Road in February 1964.

The next conversions to RM in 1964 replaced RT family vehicles on routes which had been partially converted to RM during the trolleybus replacement programme, these being the 18, 23, 64, 41 and 123. Tottenham's share of the 41 and 123 routes had remained RTW until February 1964 and both services were now all RM. Barking's allocation on the 23 had remained RT until March 1964 and Croydon's allocation on the 64 had remained RT until April. The 18 had retained a small RT allocation at Alperton until April 1964 to maintain the section of that route in the form it had operated (Edgware to Wembley Empire Pool) prior to its major daily extension in January 1962. At Barking, spare RMs on Saturdays and Sundays were used on the 169. Alperton's new RMs, its first, were also used on route 187 on Saturdays.

At Tottenham there were now enough RMs to convert route 76 on Sundays. Tottenham also received an allocation of two RMs for use on the 76 on Mondays to Fridays alongside its principal allocation of RTWs. These may have been intended for use on Brimsdown Power Station rush hour route 34B, which had no allocation of its own and took two buses from the 76 schedule for the morning and evening peaks. With the Croydon conversion of the 64, the 234 received RMs on Sundays and at Tottenham the 191 went over to RM on Saturdays.

Route 15 had been allocated RMs at weekends from January 1964, these coming from the route 7 allocation at Middle Row. In April it began to receive them all week when the major share of the route, operated by Upton Park, was converted. This conversion also involved Beckton gas works route 100, which had a limited timetable to specifically cater for workers there and their shifts. Six journeys per day operated each way on Mondays to Fridays, five on Saturdays and three on Sundays. It was not uncommon for the buses to display the 15 route number for these journeys as the schedules for the two routes were integrated. Upton Park used spare Saturday RMs from this conversion on route 169A. RM 1870 is seen in Queen Victoria Street near to Bank.

The route 30 conversion saw another modification to the RM bodywork, when part of the allocation for this route was of vehicles fitted with an offside illuminated advert display. RM 1577 was the prototype and the modification was then applied to RMs 1923 to RM 2121 and also to 100 RMLs, giving 300 vehicles in total. This form of advertising had been proposed by the British Transport Commission in 1959 but Durrant had not been keen. He consulted another major operator, the Tilling Group, who agreed with him that the proposal would present a number of technical difficulties. He also doubted that 'the illumination of adverts would be of any value in the well-lit streets of London'. They were given a trial however and may have generated some more advertising revenue. The advert panels had fallen out of use by the 1980s and were later gradually removed on surviving vehicles. The BEA Routemasters also had illuminated panels with the BEA logo, these being on the nearside above the front entrance and on the offside above the staircase panel. In both cases the panels were much narrower than on the RMs. RM 1952 is at the Roehampton terminus.

Route 106A was a Sunday only route that started to have most of its allocation converted to RM in July 1964, the Hackney share of the route using RMs that were spare on this day from the newly introduced route 30 allocation and the Dalston share coming from route 9's recent allocation. Alongside these RMs, a total scheduled allocation of 16, ran just three RTLs from Clapton. The 253B was just a renumbering of the summer Sunday only 253A, a new 253A having been introduced during the route's winter absence.

July and August 1964 saw the introduction of RMs for the Muswell Hill share of the major trunk route 134 from Potters Bar to Pimlico, with an end-to-end running time of 1 hour 35 minutes. The minority Sunday allocation on the 134A from Muswell Hill had been RM since the conversion of route 43 in June of the previous year. The Potters Bar share followed in January 1965 and then a small allocation on the route from Holloway garage a year later. RM 1966 was one of those delivered to Muswell Hill in July 1964 and is seen in Parliament Square.

With a mind to releasing the conductor from the job of supervising the platform, a front entrance version of the RML was built. It was also intended to serve as a demonstrator to provincial bus companies who had moved away by then from rear open platform buses. The special Routemaster was numbered RMF 1254 and it was delivered to London Transport in the latter part of 1962. The bus was shown at the 1962 Commercial Motor Show in October and the blinds it carried suggest it was intended to run it alongside the RMLs on route 104. The layout sacrificed three seats compared with the RML. The busmen's union, ever suspicious of London Transport's motives, prevented its use, but the layout was not well suited to one-man operation, especially in London. The design was purchased by Northern General, who bought fifty with deliveries starting in March 1964, and operated them successfully for almost 17 years. RMF 1254 was also purchased by the company in November 1966, but not before it had proved to be a useful guinea pig for the BEA airport service between the West London Air Terminal and Heathrow Airport from August 1964, a trial which resulted in an order for 65 BEA RMs with front entrances and luggage trailers.

The 130 group of routes and the Sunday only route 59 (September 1964) were next to receive RMs. That month Croydon received 32 second-hand RMs including 15 from Hendon and seven from Dalston, both of those garages getting new RMs with offside illuminated adverts in exchange. All new deliveries now had the offside illuminated advert panels and they were wanted in central London rather than Croydon and Addington. At the same time, route 197 was converted to RM on Sundays only.

In November and December 1964 another central London route received new RMs. The 137, worked by Gillingham Street and Norwood garages, received more of the illuminated advert buses, these being taken from the range RM 2031-2101. Within this range, from RM 2063 onwards, the centre relief band was extended below the destination blind, the front air intake being reduced in depth with the aim of making the buses warmer inside; how successful this was is not known. When the 137A summer Battersea Park service began in April the following year this also was RM operated. American airline Pan Am was a major early client for the offside illuminated adverts, one for that company being carried here by RM 2044. The first RMs with fleet numbers 2000 upwards had entered service in September.

On 18th November 1964 the Saturday and Sunday service on RM route 245 was diverted to replace part of the 226 route at weekends and renumbered 245A.

Route 3 from Chalk Farm garage was next for RMs, receiving them in December 1964. Norwood, which had received its first RMs with the conversion of route 137 the month before, now had further examples for the 3, which it operated in association with Chalk Farm. The ageing Norwood garage had needed some structural alterations to accommodate the RMs. RM 2064 is seen at the Camden Gardens stand at the northern end of the route on 15th December.

Opposite top: Daily route 40 received second hand vehicles in January 1965 concurrent with the revision of the service with two new variants, 40A (Monday to Friday) and 40B (Saturdays). Other routes converted to RM in 1965 using second hand buses were the 33, 45, 46, 55 and 74/A/B. These came either from service reductions or from routes 24 (converted to XA in November), 76 and 67 (converted to RML in November). Camberwell garage painted the lower half of the front air intake on some of its RMs to reflect the minor livery change introduced on new RMs at this time. RM 397 at Aldgate also has the revised radiator grille surround carried by new buses from RM 1662 in July 1963 during the conversion of route 63 and gradually retrofitted to earlier vehicles. Prototypes, minus the badge, had appeared at Shepherds Bush garage earlier that year.

Opposite: Route 5C was a new variation of route 5, taking over the 5B service on Saturdays and running from Bloomsbury to Becontree Heath. It was converted to RML just over a year later in one of the first RM to RML swaps. RM 249 is seen in Shoreditch.

With 1965 came the last routes to be converted to 64-seater RMs using brand new vehicles. These last new examples of the shorter Routemaster type were allocated to routes 6, 6A, 8 and 8A from Willesden, Bow and Hackney garages between January and May, routes 8 and 8A being the first recipients. These RMs also took over from Willesden's RTWs on route 6B, whose Walthamstow allocation had been RM since the service started. These routes mopped up over 100 RMs and their conversion took five months to complete, a process ending on 6th May 1965, just under four weeks before the RCLs began to enter service. RM 2147 is seen at Hackney Wick alongside a member of the type they replaced and RM 2115 is seen at Shoreditch.

The suffixed variants of these two major trunk routes operated over their eastern ends and thereby avoided the effect of the busiest parts of central London on their reliability. The 6A terminated at Waterloo and the 8A at London Bridge station. The two inner termini are shown in these views of RM 2208 in June 1965 and RM 2140 in April 1965. On Sundays, Bow used spare RMs on route 10, RM 2112 being seen in Stratford. Hackney's last new RMs delivered in the first week of May were 2210-2213 and 2216, all with 'flake grey' relief bands in place of the cream applied to all earlier RMs except RM 2128 at Bow, which had been the prototype for this change. This livery modification was to apply to the 400 red RMLs that were delivered after the green ones. RMs 2214, 2215 and 2217 had a delayed entry into service and 2214 was selected for an overseas trip to Tokyo. RM 2217, the highest numbered, entered service at Willesden in September along with RM 2215. RM 2214 thus became the last new RM to enter service, doing so from Riverside in February 1966. This just left initial production RM 8 as a Chiswick experimental vehicle and this did not see passenger service until as late as March 1976.

Weekend-only conversions carried out on dates not related to weekday changes of type and up to the point when delivery of new RMs was completed were as follows: the 81, which received spare 117 route RMs on Sundays from December 1962; the 116, which never had a 100% RM allocation but had a part allocation from Hounslow alongside RTs on Sundays from July 1964; the 179, on which spare Sunday RMs at Barking were used from November 1964, and Stockwell's 181, on which RMs started to be used on Sundays from October 1963.

Our story of young RMs ends in May 1965 when the last ones (2213-2217) were delivered from Park Royal. All but a handful of RMs had entered service by the end of that year and further route conversions used older vehicles displaced by new RMLs or by route changes. Exceptions that had not entered service were RM 8, the first of the production batch, which was retained by the Chiswick experimental department until 1976, and RMs 2158, 2159 and 2214, which had been on overseas tours and entered service in early 1966.

Photo Credits

Michael Beamish 57, 63 top, 105 bottom

Tony Belton 27, 28 bottom, 35, 39 both, 40, 50 bottom

James Blake 62 top, 79 top left, 100 top, 101, 111 top

Capital Transport 4, 6, 30, 73, 87, 90 bottom, 91, 92, 100 bottom, 103 top, 104 bottom right, 108 top

C Carter 11, 25 top, 34, 48 bottom, 88, 98, 99, 108 bottom

Alan B Cross 16, 23 top, 85 top, 105 top, 109 top

Michael Dryhurst 22 both, 29 top

John Gascoine 74 bottom, 78 top, 82

Ken Glazier 17 top and bottom left

Jim Hawkins collection 55

Fred Ivey 14

Peter Jones 90 top

Kevin Lane 65

W R Legg 36 top left, 43 top, 84 bottom left

Lens of Sutton 9, 15, 18 top, 21 top, 25 bottom, 26 bottom

London Transport Museum Front and back covers, 7, 8, 17 bottom right, 37 top, 42 top, 49, 56, 77, 102 bottom left, 103 bottom, 105 centre

Gerald Mead 12, 20 bottom, 67, 74 top, 75 top, 107 bottom

Peter Mitchell 1, 3, 21 bottom, 23 bottom, 24, 28 top, 29 bottom, 30 top, 31, 33, 36 bottom, 37 bottom, 38, 42 bottom, 43 bottom, 45, 48 top, 50 top, 51 both, 52 bottom, 54, 58, 59, 61, 62 bottom, 66 top, 68 both, 69 bottom, 71, 76 bottom, 79 top right, 79 bottom, 83, 84 bottom right, 85 bottom, 86, 89, 93, 94 both, 95 centre and bottom, 96 both, 104 top, 104 bottom left, 112

Alan Mortimer 52 top, 53

Robin Newell 66 bottom, 76 top

A R Packer 18 bottom, 19

Park Royal Vehicles 2 both

Malcolm Papes collection 26 top, 63 bottom, 69 top, 84 top, 95 top, 107 top, 111 bottom

Norman Rayfield, 2RT2 Preservation Group 75 bottom

Colin Stannard 79 top centre, 97, 109 bottom, 110 both

Eric Surfleet 44, 46/47, 60, 64 top, 70

Peter Thompson 80, 81

Mick Webber collection (Terry Cooper) 20 top, 64 bottom

Ron Wellings 10

Michael Wickham 32

Tony Wild 78 bottom, 106